Decorate Yourself

Cool Designs for Temporary Tattoos, Face Painting, Henna & More

Tom Andrich

Sterling Publishing Co., Inc. New York
A Sterling/Tamos Book

A Sterling/Tamos Book
© 2003 Tom Andrich

Sterling Publishing Co., Inc.
387 Park Avenue South
New York, NY 10016-8810

Tamos Books Inc.
300 Wales Avenue
Winnipeg, MB Canada R2M 2S9

10 9 8 7 6 5 4 3 2

Distributed in Canada by Sterling Publishing Co., Inc.
c/o Canadian Manda Group, One Atlantic Avenue, Suite 105
Toronto, Ontario, Canada M6K 3E7
Distributed in Great Britain by Chris Lloyd, at Orca Book Services,
Stanley House, Fleets Lane Poole, BH15 3AJ, England
Distributed in Australia by Capricorn Link (Australia) Pty Ltd.
P.O. Box 704, Windsor, NSW, 2756 Australia

Photography   Gerry Grajewski, grajewski.fotograph.inc

Printed in China

National Library of Canada Cataloguing in Publication Data

Andrich, Tom, 1945-
  Decorate yourself : cool designs for temporary tattoos, face painting,
henna & more

"A Sterling/Tamos book".
Includes index.
ISBN 1-895569-49-4

1. Face painting. 2. Body painting. 3. Temporary tattoos. I. Title.
TT911.A52 2003   745.5   C2002-910528-5

Library of Congress Cataloging-in-Publication Data

Andrich, Tom.
    Decorate yourself : cool designs for temporary tattoos, face painting, henna & more/
    Tom Andrich.
       p.cm.
     Includes index.
     ISBN 1-895569-49-4
       1. Face painting. 2. Temporary tattoos. 3. Body painting. 4. Henna. I. Title.
    TT911 .A53 2002
    745.5--dc21   2002030672

Tamos Books Inc. acknowledges the financial support of the Government of Canada through the Book Publishing Development Program
(BPIDP) for our publishing activities.

ISBN 1-895569-49-4

The zebra stencil on pp62-3 appears courtesy of Plaid Enterprises. If you are unable to locate this design you may make your own
stencil, see p 61.

The author Tom Andrich has a Bachelor of Fine Arts (BFA) degree from the University of Manitoba as well as a Teachers Certificate. He taught art in the public school system for many years but now devotes all his time to art pursuits. He works in a representational style using a variety of medium such as acrylic and oil paints, colored pencils, air brushing, charcoal, ink, pottery, clay, and welding. His subject matter is eclectic. He has exhibited at the Winnipeg Art Gallery and he instructs adults and children at the Forum Art.

Special thanks and appreciation are extended to all those who participated in making this book. Without their help and enthusiasm I could not have completed the projects.

Rebecca Andrich	Brandon Ashcroft
Suzanne Fraser	Kendall Ashcroft
Michael Fraser	Patrick Harney
Rachel-lee Tyler	Cassandra Kissick
April Neufeld	Karina Lewis
Raquel Borsos	Alana Lewis
Katie Olson	Sheri Lewis
Stephanie Imhoff	Vanessa Lewis
Laura Imhoff	Tyree Cayer
Gilllian Imhoff	Joanne Almond
Emily Miketon	Michele Keizer
Tanya Davidson	Stacy Davidson

Shahab (henna artist p 71-78) Doyawannahenna.com division of Seven Seas International
Meenu Vij from Giselle's Day Spa
Filomena Sardo from As You Like It Day Spa

Contents

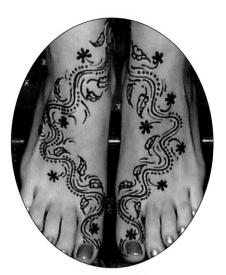
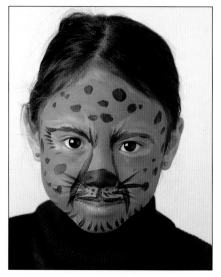
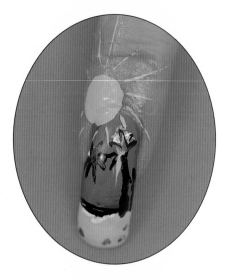

Introduction

Face and body painting is fun. Whether you use it for decoration or make-believe, to play dress-up with a costume or take part in a holiday parade, or simply to develop the ability to use a brush and paint to create a character or disguise, you can join the hundreds of happy people who enjoy this simple and rewarding art. I have painted several thousand children and adults over the past decade and taught as many more the how-to of this art, and all of them have loved it. Faces, arms, legs, backs, shoulders, ankles, even bald heads have come under my brush. The kinds of designs are endless. Children in particular like animal faces. I have studied the expressions of various animals and tried to copy their moods as well as their features and characteristics in my designs. The children add to my pleasure and their own by acting out the animal with a roar or menacing gesture. The pretend animal becomes animated and the fun is enhanced. Adding a costume only increases the mystery and disguise.

Older children and teens like body design. It's surprising how easy it is to make a flower or butterfly on a shoulder or create a snake or dragon on a cheek, arm, or leg. Over the years I have painted dozens of different body pictures — some of them quite detailed as my skills have grown and the patience of my subjects has increased. Of course, you can paint your own pictures or paint them on your friends. The great bonus is that you can erase and start again if things go wrong; however, with a little planning and practice this rarely happens.

Adults often prefer temporary tattoos and they can be made with an airbrush and paint or with henna. The henna color is harmless and natural so it does not irritate the skin. There are many simple and more complex designs for you to copy or you can make your own designs freehand. Airbrushing is a technique that can be practiced with black and colored paint. It is used with stencils and the finished designs can be sprayed with acrylic clear spray to make them last more than a day or two.

Nail art is another how-to activity that can be enjoyed by young girls, teens, and adults. With some nail polish and paint you can create painted fingernails or toenails with lovely abstract designs, figures, or scenes that are sure to attract admiration. Add some tiny jewels, some movable eyes, or some gel to give dimension to your spectacular projects. As you begin, it's easy to copy the designs from the instructions given. As you progress, you'll want to create your own masterpieces.

Can anyone create this painting magic? Absolutely! In the following pages I have outlined all the techniques and equipment needed to make hundreds of painted designs. I've included patterns and stencil-making instructions as well as pictures for you to copy. With a little practice you can produce this special fun entertainment to share with family and friends.

Face and Body Painting

Equipment

You will need a variety of supplies to complete your face and body painting designs. They can be purchased in different price ranges, but the ones I use are moderately priced and readily available in toy stores, art supply stores, specialty hobby shops, theatrical supply stores, and some department stores. Be sure to have the proper materials on hand before you begin your project. See photo at right.

Setting Up

Choose a comfortable chair – a regular size folding lawn chair works well for the painter. Use a low TV table with legs to place beside the lawn chair on the side of your painting arm. The person to be painted sits facing the painter at a distance comfortable for the painter to reach. A child's folding lawn chair is a good choice for this because it puts the subject at the right height and position to be painted.

Paints

Water-base makeup produces a professional finish and is easier to use than gouache, tempera, and acrylic paints or water soluble crayons (wax crayons are not suitable for face painting). I use a water-base theater makeup. It is available at theater and hobby shops as well as art stores. It can be applied with a brush or sponge and spreads evenly over the face or body surface. It contains enough oil to keep the paint flexible on the skin, which is important for more natural expression and movement and it doesn't flake off.

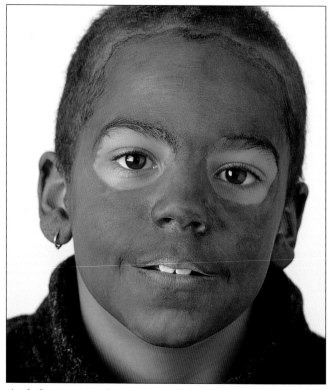

Apply base coat evenly over face

 Water-base paint comes in 18 ml plastic containers that may crack before the paint is used up. To prevent this transfer the paints into the cups of a small plastic muffin tray or suitable divided container. This face paint is also available in small face painting kits with limited colors. You can purchase additional color cakes separately as you need them or use the primary colors and mix your own shades. Follow the color chart for color direction. To mix, I select the brush, dip it in the first color and put it on the palette. Then I clean the brush in water and dip it in the second color and transfer this to the first color on the palette. Mix the two with the brush. Add a little of one color or the other until you get the shade you need.

Note This paint washes off easily with warm water and soap. Try not to get it on clothing because some colors may stain.

Mix red and white paint to make pink

Color Chart

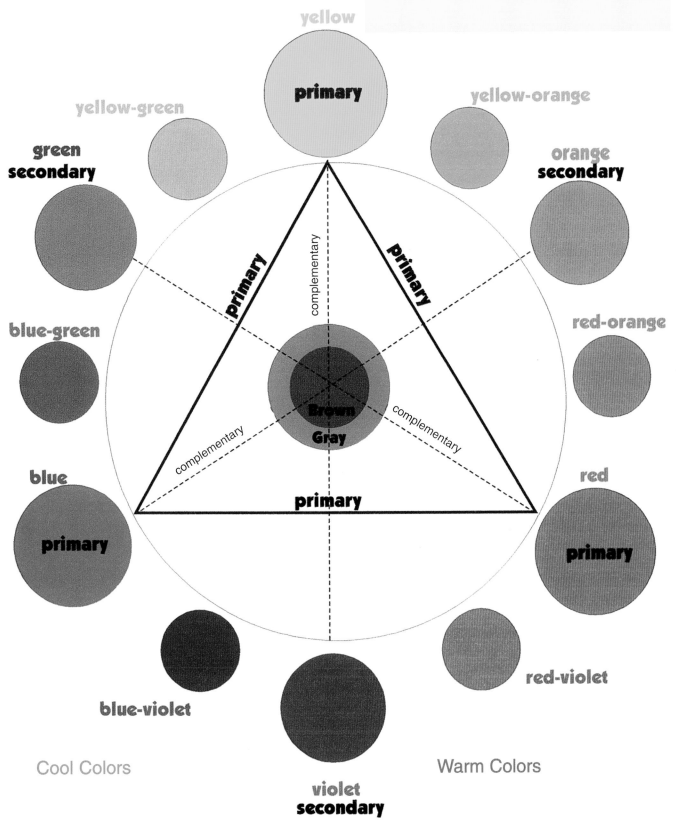

yellow
primary

yellow-green

yellow-orange

**green
secondary**

orange
secondary

blue-green

red-orange

primary **primary**

complementary

Brown
Gray

complementary complementary

blue

primary

red

primary

primary

red-violet

blue-violet

Cool Colors

Warm Colors

violet
secondary

Water Jar

Use a shallow, wide-mouthed plastic jar filled with water to wet and clean brushes and sponges. Change water frequently. Use paper towels to clean and dry brushes.

Brushes

To paint details on face or body, good quality synthetic water color brushes are effective and inexpensive. I use sizes 1 or 2 round, 5 or 6 round, 8, 9, or 10 round, and ¾ in flat. This is a minimum requirement. You may wish to add others according to the details of your painting.

Brushes lose their points from the oils on the skin and constant abrasion and need to be replaced after a while. Brush tubes, that can be purchased for the brushes, help to prolong the life of the brush. After use, wash the brush thoroughly, allow to dry, and store in the tube.

To paint larger areas I use a sponge brush (p 16) that comes with a wooden handle. Pieces of foam cut in 1 in or 3 in wedges can also be used. Use a different foam wedge or brush for each different color. Rinse well after use and dry before storing. These brushes can be purchased at paint or home building stores.

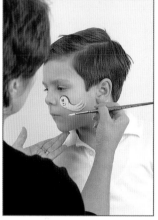

Hold brush in writing hand

Press down to make a wide stroke

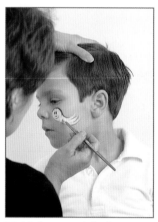

Hold child's chin so paint strokes will be even

Hold the top of the head to keep the child from moving back

Makeup Fixative

Sometimes children like the painted design so much they want it to last for a while. If the design is sprayed with an acrylic medium or clear spray fixative and allowed to dry, the design will last longer. This is quite effective with airbrush designs, which may last for 2 or 3 days as long as they are not rubbed directly. I **never** spray on the face for fear of getting it in the eyes. You can purchase clear acrylic in a spray can at art or paint stores.

How to Paint

Hold the brush firmly in your writing hand, (as shown in top photo, opposite page). When you press down on a quality brush and release it, the hairs will spring back into position. This enables you to do a variety of strokes, from a thin line to wide line. To achieve a fluid stroke the paint needs to be thinned with water, and judging how much water to use requires practice.

Wet the brush completely and dip it into the paint for an overall color. For a fine line, wet only the tip of the brush in water and remove excess water on the side of the jar. Dip tip of brush in paint and make the fine line. Steady your painting hand by resting the little finger on the face or body of the person you are painting (see photo opposite).

All children move their heads back as soon as the painting begins. Use your non-painting hand to hold the child's chin or place it on top of the child's head (see photo on opposite page). This steadies the child and prevents any unwanted color streaks across the face or any accidental contact with the eyes.

Wet the brush completely and wipe it on the side of the water jar

Dip brush completely in paint

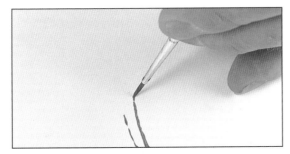

To paint a fine line wet only the tip of the brush, dip tip in paint, and paint with tip of brush only

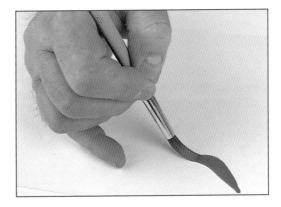

Draw the brush flat across the skin for a wide stroke

Face Painting Steps

1 Apply base coat (all over face design area) with 1 in foam brush. Keep enough paint on the brush for good coverage.

2 Leave space around eyes or anywhere darker paint will be applied (eg whiskers, eyebrow areas).

3 Apply paint with light pressure to avoid streaks.

4 If streaks are required, make them in the direction of the contours of the head.

5 Apply dark color first, then lighter color, then fine black lines last.

6 If light colors go on top of dark colors (scales opposite page), brush on lightly to avoid mixing with color underneath.

7 To paint whiskers, place three or four rows of dots where the whiskers grow. With smallest round brush start the stroke at the dot and taper the stroke to a thin tip.

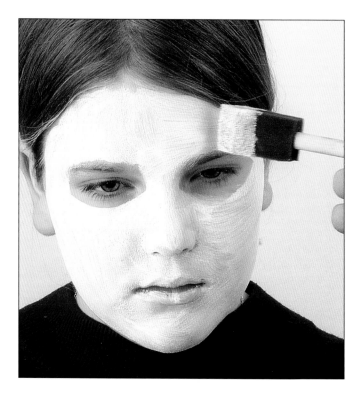

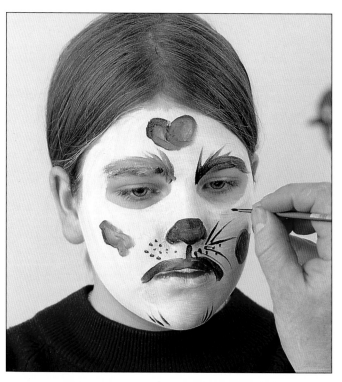

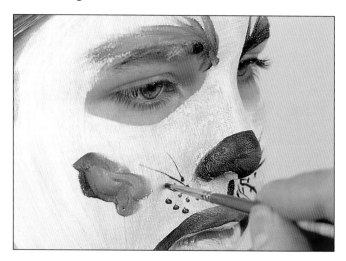

Saftey Tips

Safety Tips

1 Be sure to leave uncolored space around the eyes. If any color accidentally gets in the eyes, remove excess color around the eye with tissue and rinse the eye with clean water.

2 Never use glitter or sequins around the eyes or face. They could scratch the eyes.

3 Water-base paints are usually non-allergenic and any adverse reaction to them is extremely rare. If the paint causes a rash or itchy skin on face or body,or watery eyes, remove the paint immediately with warm water and soap.

4 If you are painting many different people, you might want to clean brushes in a weak solution of disinfectant (4 parts water to 1 part chlorine bleach) or alchohol.

5 When handling brushes be sure to keep pointed ends away from eyes.

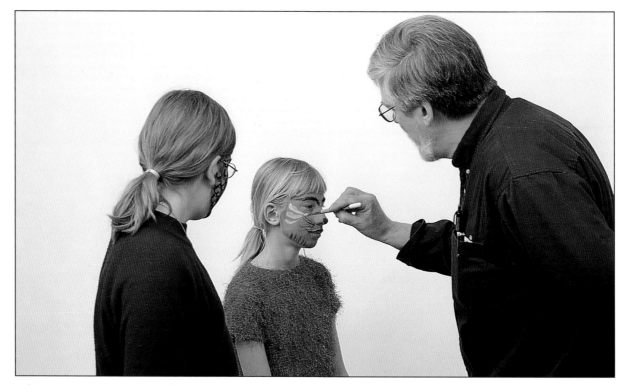

When you are painting more than one person be sure to disinfect brushes

When applying base coat keep hair off face

Apply eyebrows with full brush strokes

Apply gray base coat for owl

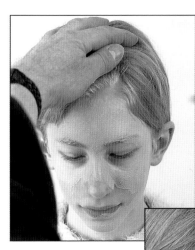

Apply yellow paint, then black, then white. Allow each color to dry thoroughly.

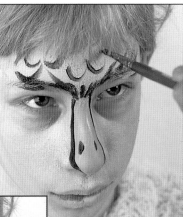

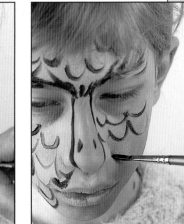

Face Painting Fun

Having your face painted is fun. The paint washes off quickly so if you make a mistake it's easy to begin again. Sometimes mistakes turn out to be creative steps to a new design, so if your painting is different from the picture that's all right. When you're having your face painted, it's best to wear clothing that can be washed, just in case there are spills. If you plan to use the painted face as part of a costume, put on the costume before your face is painted so you won't have to pull anything over the painted face and smear the paint. The painter should read all the instructions before beginning the design and have all the equipment and materials at hand. The subject's hair should be tied or pinned back off the face before the painting begins.

For a special costume dress-up add a blue star and dot patch to basic clown face makeup on opposite page. Using medium brush, paint white teeth on lower lip (shown above).

HAPPY CLOWN

1 Using the sponge brush and white paint, cover the entire face except the space for the eyebrows, mouth, and red nose (top photo).

2 Using the medium brush and red paint, fill in the eyebrows, mouth, and nose. Paint on red freckles and red circle patch (center photo) on cheek.

3 Use the smallest brush and black paint to make lines under red eyebrows and in the corners of the mouth to accent upper curve of mouth (bottom photo).

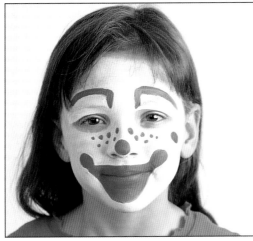

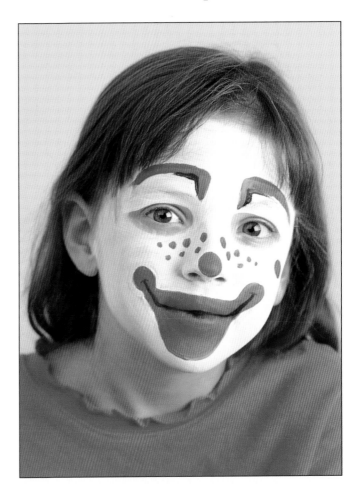

21

TIGER

1 Using the sponge brush and orange paint, cover the face, leaving areas around the eyebrows, under the nose and chin, unpainted (top photo).

2 Using the largest brush and white paint, fill in the white eyebrows using press and release tapering strokes, beginning at the subject's natural eyebrows and continuing for a curve effect around the eyebrow. Now paint in white using the same brush stroke beginning at base of nose and continuing outward. Paint under the jaw using the same brush stroke beginning under the jaw and continuing up toward the cheek (center photo).

3 Using the largest brush and black paint, make stripes across the forehead, along the temples, and on the cheeks. The stripes should be a little wiggly to look more realistic. With a tapered stroke, paint black lines on the eyebrow ridge. Paint a black line under the nose to the lip and follow the lip, then curve up slightly. Paint nose black. Using the smallest brush and black paint, make small black dots for the whiskers — paint the whiskers. With the same brush paint a series of tapered strokes starting under the jaw and finishing under the cheeks (bottom photo). Outline teeth.

4 Use the small brush and black paint to emphasize the chin lines, leaving some lines fine and making some lines heavier.

SPACE SPIDER

1 Using the sponge brush and light yellow paint cover the face as shown in top photo. Leave a space around the eyes. Use the medium brush and white paint to fill in the white space around the eyes, being careful not to paint too close to the eyes (top photo).

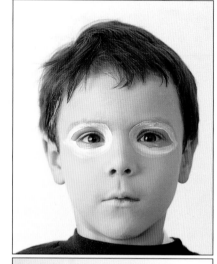

2 Using the smallest brush and black paint begin making the face lines. Begin at the nose and proceed to the side of the head. Make the lines symmetrical on each side of the face, as shown (center photo). Make the spider at the end of the nose.

3 Using the same brush and black paint make a series of curved lines in between the long lines you have completed. Make sure the curved lines connect with the long lines, as shown in the bottom photo.

GRAY OWL

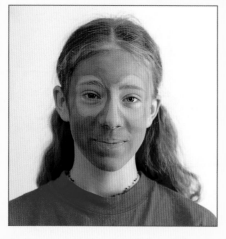

1 Using the sponge brush and gray paint cover the face leaving the area around the eyes and down the nose unpainted, as shown in top photo. Using the smallest brush and yellow paint, fill in the area down the nose and around the eyes, being careful not to come too close to the eyes.

2 Using the small brush and black paint, make an outline around the eye circles and around the yellow on the nose. Make 2 dots on the nose and a few small lines at the top of yellow nose color (see center photo).

The feathers require a special technique. Using the largest round brush and black paint make single curved strokes over the gray paint on the face. This gives the feathers a realistic appearance. Using the same brush and black paint, make thick curved marks above and below each eye.

3 Using the largest round brush and light gray paint make curved strokes above the black feather strokes and make upward strokes above the yellow nose patch, as shown in bottom photo.

CALICO CAT

1 Using the sponge brush and yellow paint cover the face, leaving the nose area unpainted (top photo).

2 Using a medium brush and black paint make the eyebrows using long tapered brush strokes. Paint the dots for the whiskers under the nose. Paint whisker strokes along the jaw line and sweeping strokes up from the whisker dots (center photo).

3 Using a medium brush and light blue paint make the nose and paint blue strokes along the whisker lines, between the whiskers, and up from the eyebrows.

PRINCESS

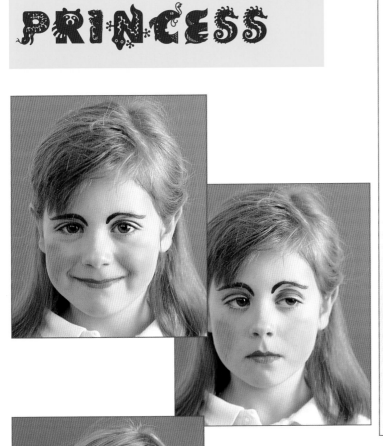

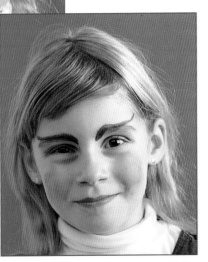

For a party or Halloween, a princess costume is a favorite. You can make the costume or purchase one ready-made and make up a princess face to match.

1 Using a medium brush and green or blue paint, make a line along the fold of the eyelid.

2 Using the sponge brush dab lightly into the red color and paint the cheeks, trying not to make streaks. Painting with a circular motion is usually best.

3 Using the small brush and red color, paint the lips.

4 Using the medium brush and black paint, make the eyebrows, curving them up at the ends.

WOLF

1 Using the sponge brush and gray paint, cover the face, leaving areas around the eyes, end of nose, and mouth unpainted. Do not paint the eyelids (top photo).

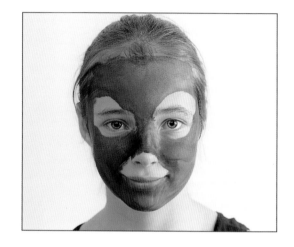

2 Using a medium brush and gray paint, make a thick line from the nose to the upper lip, and color the upper lip gray as well. With the largest round brush and black paint cover the entire end of the nose, and make black lines for the eyebrows and black strokes on the chin (center photo).

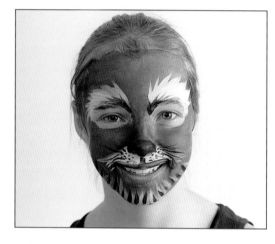

3 Using the medium brush and white paint fill in the eyebrow area and the area under the nose. Make white strokes beside the black thin strokes. Make the fangs with one stroke of white. Make some white lines across the nose, as shown.

Using the smallest brush and black paint, make black whisker dots under the nose. Using the same brush make the whiskers beginning at the black dots and sweeping outward to the cheeks (bottom photo).

SNAKE

1 Using the sponge brush and green paint, cover the face leaving an area around the eyes and the lips unpainted (top photo).

2 Using the largest brush and light green paint, make curved strokes in a pattern over the face (center photo).

3 Using a medium brush and black paint make short curved strokes under each of the light green strokes. If you wish to enhance the light green scales, give each scale another stroke of light green color (bottom left photo).

4 Using the smallest brush paint a red forked tongue for the snake and outline the tongue with black paint (bottom photo).

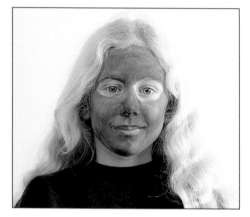

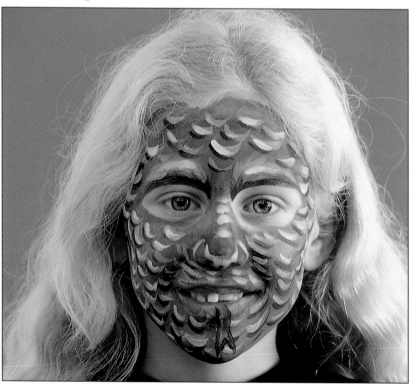

The snake and the lizard painted faces are much the same and they can be made as menacing and scary as the painter wishes.

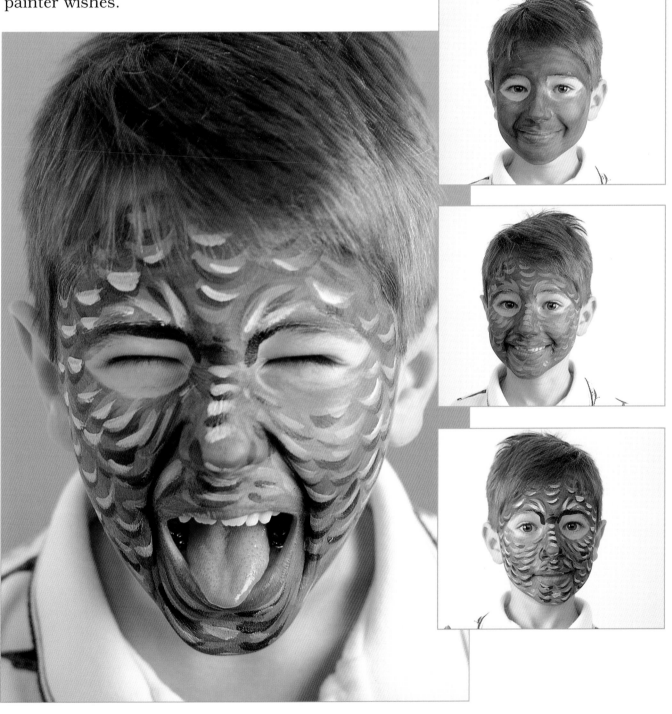

Pirates—with a sword and eye patch—look very threatening. This young pirate is ready for any adventure, especially trick or treating! It's easy to make or purchase costume that complements the elaborate face painting of this make-believe buccaneer.

1 Using the largest brush and black paint make eyebrows with sweeping upward strokes. Then paint a black circle around one eye and paint a line from patch across forehead and from patch to temple. Also paint black mustache and beard, as shown in top photo.

2 Using medium brush and gray paint make small brush strokes over the beard, mustache, and eyebrows.

3 Using the smallest brush and red paint, make a series of small stitch strokes for a scar across the cheek and on the nose (bottom right photo).

RACCOON

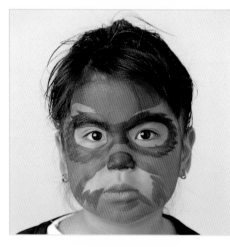

1 Using the sponge brush and brown paint, cover the face, leaving the eyebrows, around the eyes, upper lip areas unpainted (top photo).

2 Using the largest brush and white paint, fill in the eyebrows, mustache area, and white strokes on chin. Using the same brush and black paint, make the eye mask and nose (center photo).

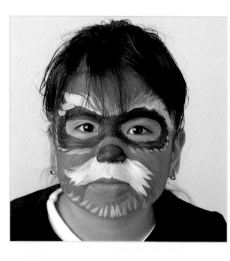

3 Using a medium brush and black paint, make black dots on upper lip area. Make whisker lines beginning at dots and tapering to a thin point. Make a fat black line from nose to upper lip and along lip line. Make black brush strokes between white strokes along chin (bottom photo).

4 Using same brush and white paint, make small stokes under eye mask.

SAD CLOWN

1 Using the large sponge brush and white paint, cover face, leaving space around eyes, eyebrow areas, end of nose, and top of lip area unpainted (top photo).

2 With large round brush and red paint, fill in downturned mouth area and end of nose (center photo).

3 With medium brush and blue paint, fill in eyebrows. Make teardrops under the eyes. Using the smallest brush and black paint, make lines at the corners of the mouth to emphasize the turned down look. Add the costume and you're ready for a great party.

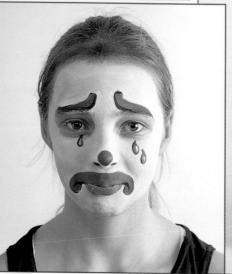

CHEETAH

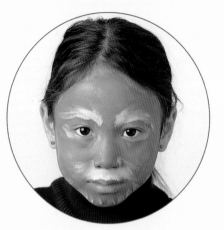

1 Using the large sponge brush and yellow-ocher, paint the entire face, leaving space around the eyes unpainted. With medium brush and white paint, make sweeping brush strokes above eyebrows, along mustache area, and wide strokes along chin line (above).

2 Using medium brush and black paint make cheetah spots over face, as shown. Paint black eyebrows and line running from eyebrows along sides of nose (above photo).

3 Using the same brush paint a black nose, lines from the sides of nose along sides of mouth, and line from under nose to upper lip and along lip line. Paint black strokes along chin line. Using smallest brush and black paint make dots on upper lip area and paint tapering lines from dots for whiskers (above).

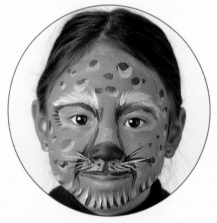

4 Using medium brush and blue paint make curved strokes under the black spots. Using the same brush and white paint, make curved strokes under the blue strokes. Make white strokes between the black whiskers strokes on chin line (above).

This T-rex painted face looks as menacing as the giant creature itself. It's great fun for Halloween or any other dress-up party.

1 Using a sponge brush and dark green paint, cover the face and ears, leaving space around the eyes and the lips unpainted (below).

2 Using the medium brush and white paint, make the white teeth.

3 Using the medium brush and black paint, make curved brush strokes over the face and nose for scales (bottom left).

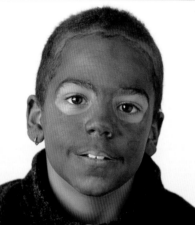

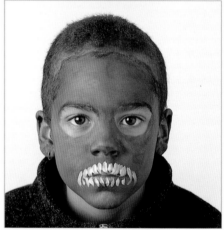

4 Using a medium brush and light green paint, make curved brush strokes above the black strokes to highlight the scales (bottom right).

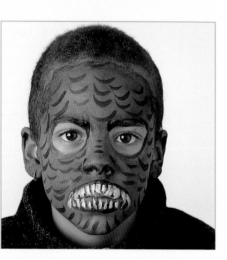

BUTTERFLY

1 Using the smallest brush and mauve paint, draw the outline of the wings so they are even on each side of the nose. The nose will be the butterfly body. Using the same paint and the largest brush, fill in the outline, leaving the space around the eyes and center of the nose unpainted, as shown (at left).

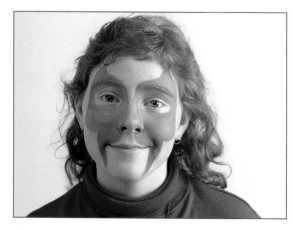

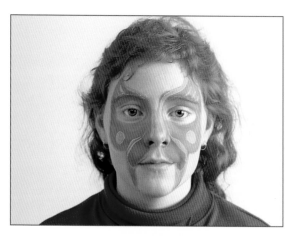

2 Using the medium brush and blue paint, make a thick outline around the mauve area and paint 2 blue dots on the cheeks, as shown, right, and blue curved lines under the eyes and over the eyebrows.

3 Using the medium brush and black paint, fill in the body of the butterfly and paint the antennae. Paint black lines around the wings, as shown, and a line on each nostril.

1 Using the sponge brush and white paint, cover the face, leaving the eye area, tip of nose, and around the eyes unpainted, at left.

2 Using the largest brush and black paint, color the nose, make friendly curved eyebrows, and a mouth that turns down at the ends (cats' mouths turn up). Make black dots on upper lip and lines on chin with smallest brush.

3 Using the smallest brush and black paint, begin at each dot and draw a fine line outward for the whiskers with largest brush make black patches on face.

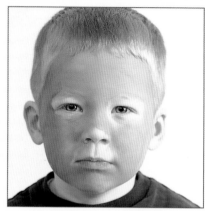

1 Using the sponge brush and dark yellow paint, cover the face, leaving space around the eye area, and the nose, and upper lip unpainted (above).

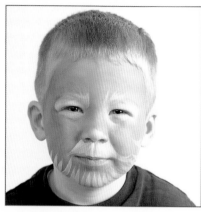

2 Using the largest brush and light yellow paint, fill in the area under the nose, stroke along the jaw line, and the tapered eyebrows (above).

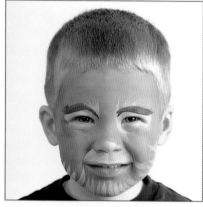

3 Using the medium brush and brown paint, make straight-across eyebrows, as shown above.

4 Using the medium brush and black paint, make a black line under the eyebrows, color the nose, make a black line from the nose to the upper lip, and across upper lip. Make black strokes along chin line, as shown above.

5 Using smallest brush and black paint, make dots along upper lip and paint a line from the dots, curving up. With white paint make 2 large teeth, as shown, and outline them in black on one side, as shown above.

46

RABBIT

1 Using the sponge brush and white paint cover the entire face leaving eye area and lips unpainted (above photo).

2 Using the large sponge brush and a little red paint on the tip, apply it to the cheeks with a light, circular motion (above photo).

3 Using the medium brush and red paint, apply it to the tip of the nose, allowing the white to mix with the red for a pink color. Using the same brush and black paint, make the arched eyebrows and add sweeping strokes for bushy eyebrows. Outline two large teeth, and make a line from nose to upper lip and a line for the upper lip. Using the smaller brush paint black dots under the nose and make a tapering line from each dot for whiskers. Add a few whiskers under eyes and on chin, as shown. Using white paint, fill in the teeth again, to emphasize the color (above photo).

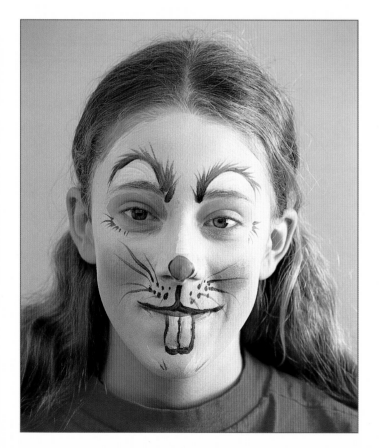

It's always special to have a design painted on your face or some other part of your body. This fun can be arranged for a birthday party, school play, or any other special event. If you practice ahead of time you can paint a design on yourself and your friends, or perhaps you can persuade Mom or another family member to paint a favorite bird or animal on each member of your group as you head off to a fair or the amusement park. Spraying the design with fixative will prevent smears and make it last longer. This works well for arms and legs but not on the face because it may get into the eyes. When spraying another person ask the person to turn the head away while you spray. Spray with short bursts. If you are spraying many images you should wear a mask.

Painting Techniques

These smaller designs usually require smaller lines and details. I use the smallest and medium size round brushes and less water on the brush as I paint. It's easiest to apply dark colors first, allow to dry, and then apply light colors on top. After you have painted in all the colors you then outline the design with a fine black line using the finest brush. This requires a steady hand and you'll need to brace your painting arm with your other hand so you won't have wobbly lines.

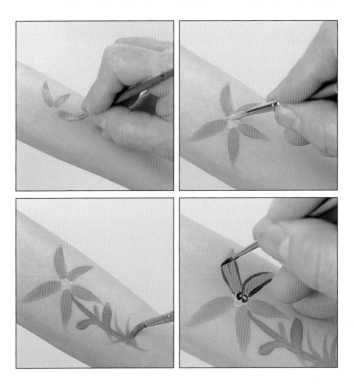

1 Using the medium brush, mix the pink paint (red + white) on your palette (p 12).

2 Paint 5 flower petals. Clean brush.

3. Using yellow paint, make flower center. Clean brush.

4 Using green paint make a stem and leaves. Clean brush.

5 Using white paint make light brush strokes on petals. Clean brush.

6 Using the finest brush and black paint, make a fine line around the petals and around the flower center.

Body Designs

Pumpkin

1 Using medium brush and orange paint, make pumpkin shape.

2 Using fine brush and black paint, make lines on pumpkin.

3 Using the same brush draw green lines for grass under pumpkin and vines around pumpkin.

Rudolph

1 Using black paint and fine brush, outline reindeer head and antlers. Make eye and eyelid. Mark line for mouth and outline nose and insets for ears.

2 With medium brush and brown paint fill in head, neck, and antlers.

3 With same brush and white paint, fill in nose area, ears, eye space, and patch below neck.

4 Using fine brush and red paint, fill in nose and shine marks.

Rainbow

1 Using medium brush and red, orange, yellow, green, blue, purple paints make successive streaks of color, as shown.

2 Using fine brush and black paint outline a pot of gold under rainbow. Add gold pieces in pot.

3 Using fine brush and gold/yellow paint, fill in pot and coins.

4 With medium brush and green paint, make grass strokes under pot.

5 With fine brush and black paint make handle lines on pot.

6 With same brush and black paint make hightlight lines on pot.

7 With same brush and white paint make shine lines around pot of gold.

Heart

1 Using fine brush and black paint, outline heart.

2 Using medium brush and red paint, fill in heart.

3 Using fine brush and white paint, draw scalloped edge around heart. Make highlight marks on heart.

Planets

1 Using medium brush and yellow paint begin the swirls for the sun. With the same brush and orange paint finish the swirls for the sun.

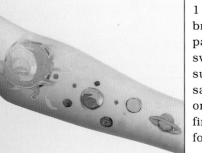

2 Using fine brush and blue paint make the earth and 2 other planets. Darken the blue paint and finish the earth.

3 With the same brush and turqoise paint make another planet.

4 With the fine brush and light brown paint make the final planet. Use black paint to outline planet and rings. Make Sun, Mercury, Venus, Earth, Mars, Jupiter, Saturn, Uranus, Neptune, and Pluto.

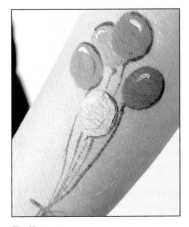

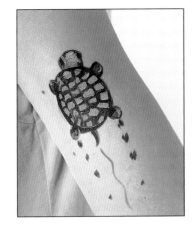

Balloons

1 Using red paint and medium brush color one balloon.

2 Repeat with yellow, blue, green paint and mauve paint for other balloons.

3 Using black paint and fine brush, make outline of 5 balloons and strings.

4 Using white paint and fine brush make highlights on balloons.

Dinosaur

1 Using fine brush and black paint, outline dinosaur.

2 Using fine brush and green paint fill in dinosaur, draw trees with brown paint.

3 Using same brush and green paint, make leaves and grass.

4 Using fine brush and white paint, make dinosaur tummy.

Turtle

1 Using fine brush and black paint, draw outline of turtle, make tail.

2 Using medium brush and green paint fill in turtle shape.

3 Using fine brush and black paint, make section marks on back of turtle, make eyes.

4 Using brown paint make trail marks in sand.

Flower Bouquet

1 Using medium brush and turqoise paint make cluster of flowers.

2 Using same brush and green paint, fill in leaves around flowers.

3 Using same brush and turqoise paint make 3 more flowers above leaves.

4 Using same brush and pink paint, make flowers above turqoise flowers and one beside lower turquoise flowers.

5 Using fine brush and black paint, make center of flowers.

Lizard

1 Using fine brush and black paint, draw outline of the lizard.

2 Using medium brush and green paint fill in lizard.

3 Using fine brush and black paint, make tiny lines on lizard skin and redefine claws.

4 Using the same brush and white paint make the eyes.

5 Using the same brush and brown paint make the bug and footprints in the sand.

Masks

1 Using black paint and fine brush, make outline of masks.

2 Using white paint and medium brush, fill in masks.

3 Using black paint and fine brush, draw in eyes, eyebrows, nostrils, mouth (one happy, one sad).

4 Using fine brush and blue paint, draw strings from masks.

5 Using fine brush and blue paint, outline some lines.

Bunch of Flowers

1 Using medium brush and pink paint, color large flowers pink and small flowers blue.

2 Using black paint and fine brush, draw the outline of 3 large flowers and 2 small flowers.

3 Using same brush and green paint, draw in leaf shapes and color them.

4 Using fine brush and orange paint, make center of flower.

5 Using the same brush and black paint make an area around part of flower centers and make defining marks to highlight leaves.

Single Flower

1 Using medium brush and pink paint, fill in flower.

2 Using fine brush and black paint outline 5 petals of flower, center of flower, and stem.

3 Using same brush and green paint, go over black stem and add leaves.

4 Using fine brush and orange paint, make center of flower.

5 Using same brush and white paint, make highlights on flower petals.

White Daisy

1 Using fine brush and white paint make daisy petals for 3 flowers.

2 Using same brush and orange paint, make center of flowers.

3 Using the same brush and green paint make the stems and leaves.

4 Using the same brush and black paint add highlights to stems and leaves, centers of flowers, and petals.

Pink Bear

1 Using fine brush and black paint outline the bear and 2 balloons, as shown.

2 Using the medium brush and pink paint, fill in bear and one balloon.

3 Using the same brush and blue paint, color bear's top and other balloon.

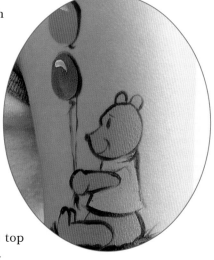

4 Using fine brush and black paint make eyes, nose, mouth, and sleeve marks on top.

Mouse

1 With medium brush and gray paint fill in mouse color.

2 Using fine brush and black paint outline mouse shape.

3 Using fine brush and black paint make eyes and nose, define limbs and mouth.

4 Using fine brush and orange paint make cheese.

5 Using same brush and green paint make grass strokes.

Ghost

1 Using medium brush and white paint fill in ghost.

2 Using fine brush and black paint outline ghost shape.

3 Using fine brush and black paint make eyes and features and heavy line over head.

Starfish

1 Using medium brush and orange paint fill in star. With darker orange paint make spines of starfish. With lighter orange paint make added spines to starfish.

2 Using fine brush and black paint outline the starfish

Hummingbird

1 Using medium brush and blue paint, fill in bird color.

2 Using fine brush and black paint outline hummingbird.

3 Using same brush paint white breast.

4 Using fine brush and black paint, make wing marks, tail marks, and eye.

Unicorn

1 With medium brush and white paint color in head and make flowing strokes for mane.

2 Using fine brush and black paint outline unicorn head, horn, and lines of mane.

3 Using fine brush and black paint add eye, nostril, and mouth. Touch up ears and tail.

4 Using same brush and gray paint add highlight strokes, as shown.

Snake

1 Using fine brush and green paint color snake.

2 Using fine brush and black paint outline snake form.

3 Using same brush and black paint make scales, eye, mouth.

4 Using same brush and orange paint make tongue.

Panda

1 Using fine brush and black paint outline a panda bear.

2 With medium brush and black paint fill in arms and legs.

3 Using the same brush and white paint, fill in other parts of the panda.

4 Using fine brush and black paint, draw in face and other lines of panda.

5 With same brush and green paint, make grass strokes under panda and grass stem.

Elephant

1 Using fine brush and gray paint fill in elephant shape.

2 Using fine brush and black paint, outline an elephant form.

3 Using fine brush and brown paint make tree trunks.

4 With medium brush and dark green paint make trees and grass.

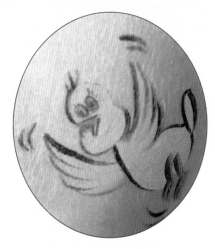

Christmas Trees

1. Using green paint and medium brush, make tree shapes.

2 Using black or dark green paint and medium brush, make defining marks on trees.

3 Using brown paint and fine brush, make small trees in background.

4 Using fine brush and white paint, draw snow on and under trees.

5 Using fine brush and light green paint, highlight some branches.

Yellow Bird

1 Using medium brush and yellow paint, fill in bird shape.

2 Using black paint and fine brush, outline yellow bird and marks around bird, eyes, beak, and legs.

3 Using fine brush and orange paint fill in beak, legs, eyes, and go over marks around bird.

Bat

1 Using fine brush and black paint make outline of bat and fill in color.

2 With fine brush and yellow paint make moon.

3 With same brush and gray paint make clouds across moon.

Rose

1 Using fine brush and red paint, fill in rose and bud.

2 Using fine brush and black paint, outline rose petals, stems, and bud.

3 Using same brush and green paint, go over stems and add leaves.

AirBrush Tattoos

These temporary tattoos are colorful and fun. You can wear one on your arm or ankle, or both, and by the time you are tired of it, it will have disappeared. I used airbrushing and stencils as well as some hand-painted details to make these tattoos and then sprayed them with acrylic clear spray. A design can last up to two or three days if no direct water or abrasion are applied.

Airbrushing is used for a number of techniques such as illustration and photo retouching. It requires special equipment and some acquired skill for operation. For my purposes I have chosen a relatively inexpensive Pasche VL model which comes with three different size needles for various thicknesses of paint. I prefer the simple single-action model which means that you control the air and the paint with one trigger press down for the air at the same time pulling back for the paint flow. The air is supplied by a compressor (generally manufactured to go with the airbrush). I prefer a moderately priced oilless compressor with a reserve tank. The air pressure you need is between 20 pounds and 40 pounds depending on the thickness of the paint and how close you are spraying.

There are paints specifically made to use in an airbrush (acrylic and latex paints need to be thinned and even then may be too thick and clog the airbrush). Airbrush paints come ready to spray in a variety of colors that are easy to mix for a wide array of shades. You can also purchase an airbrush medium with which to thin the paint in the bottles so you can fill these with the paint you need and switch them as the color is needed for your design. Be sure to have a cover on the cups so the paint does not spill out. If there is no cover, a piece of masking tape will work, but leave a tiny hole in the top for air pressure.

An airbrush requires some care and cleaning. When you have finished using it you can immediately submerge it in a pail of water. If this is not possible, take it apart and clean the needle by running water through it (I carry a water bottle with a spout for this purpose).

Airbrush Method

The method I use to airbrush tattoos is simple and quick. I use black paint in the airbrush to spray the outline using a stencil, and hand paint in the color. You can use various colored airbrush paint or you can mix your own color. Using a clean brush put the colors you want to mix in a baby food jar or plastic film canister. Use the color chart on p 13 as a color mix guide.

How to Airbrush
Airbrush painting is easy to do but requires some practice to feel comfortable with the technique. Use a low pressure when spraying tattoos. If you spray too close the paint will run, if too far away the body design will be too light and you will overspray on to clothing. See photo below.

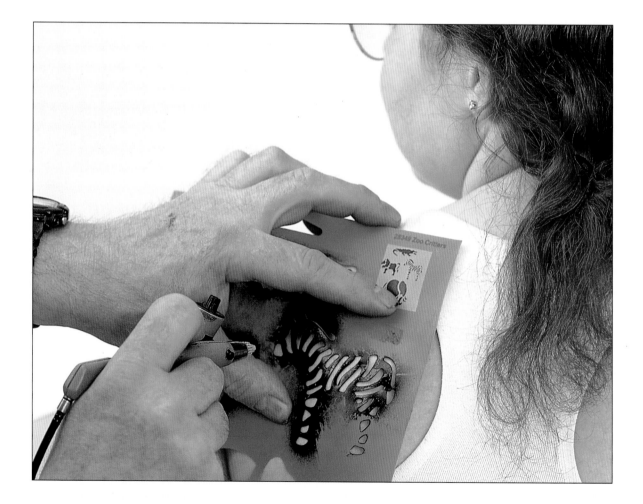

Making Stencils for Airbrushing

Using stencils makes airbrushing tattoos easier to apply. There are a variety of stencils available at art stores and hobby shops or you can make your own from the patterns in this book (p 64-6). You will need a stencil cutter (electric or butane), mylar or overhead projector sheets, a piece of heavy glass 8 in x 10 in, masking tape, and the pattern. NOTE Stencils may also be cut with an xacto knife, but this is dangerous and not recommended here.

1 Plug in the stencil cutter about 10 - 15 minutes before use so it will be hot enought to cut easily.

2 Photocopy the stencil pattern from the book.

3 Place the stencil on a flat surface and place the glass sheet over top.

4 Place the mylar over the glass and tape in place with masking tape.

5 Trace along the outline of the areas you want to be filled in with spray. These parts will be cut out.

6 Lift off the mylar sheet and your stencil will be visible. Place the stencil pattern on the subject. Put black paint in the paint cup of the airbrush.

7 Next, begin spraying with the airbrush (p 60). The paint will color only those areas of the pattern that are cut out. I use black paint to make the basic design. If you wish to spray the image with multiple colors you can put other colors in additional paint cups or wash out the cup and airbrush for each change of color. However, you should cut a stencil for each different color layer you wish to use. See p 63. I use a brush to hand paint other colors into the image with face paints or acrylic paint.

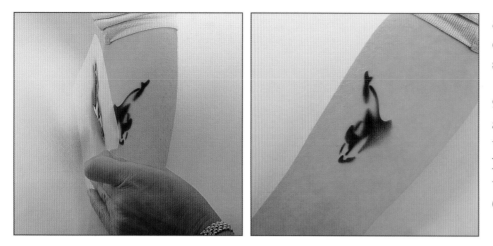

8 Remove the stencil carefully and allow the skin coloring to dry.

9 I use black paint for airbrushing. The image transferred to the arm here is black. To finish the image in color see p 63.

Stick-on Transfers

There are other ways to transfer images to the skin. You can purchase patterns which you press on the skin and a pattern outline remains when the pattern is lifted off. The image outline is in black and this can be filled in with black paint for a black image tattoo which many people prefer. Or the image outline may be filled in with colored paint. These transfer tattoos can be made to last longer by spraying them with a fixative or hair spray.

How to Color

The black paint I use in my airbrush produces a well defined image and many people prefer this as the final image for the tattoo.

1 Place the stencil on the skin

2 Spray the image.

3 Carefully remove the stencil.

4 Allow the chosen stencil image to dry (zebra here).

5 You may use the black image as the finished tattoo or you can paint it.

Painting Stencil Images

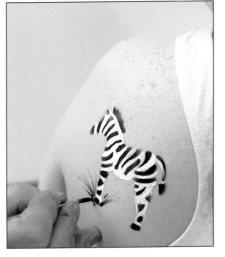

6 Using the medium brush and white paint, fill in the unsprayed areas making a precise and neat body design. Paint black eyes, hooves, and nose. Allow to dry.

7 Using the same brush and green paint, make some grass strokes beneath the zebra.

8 You can add as many artistic touches as you wish.

9 Spray the image with fixative. Hold the subject's arm or leg away from the body and turn the face away. Spray lightly and allow to dry.

Stencil Patterns

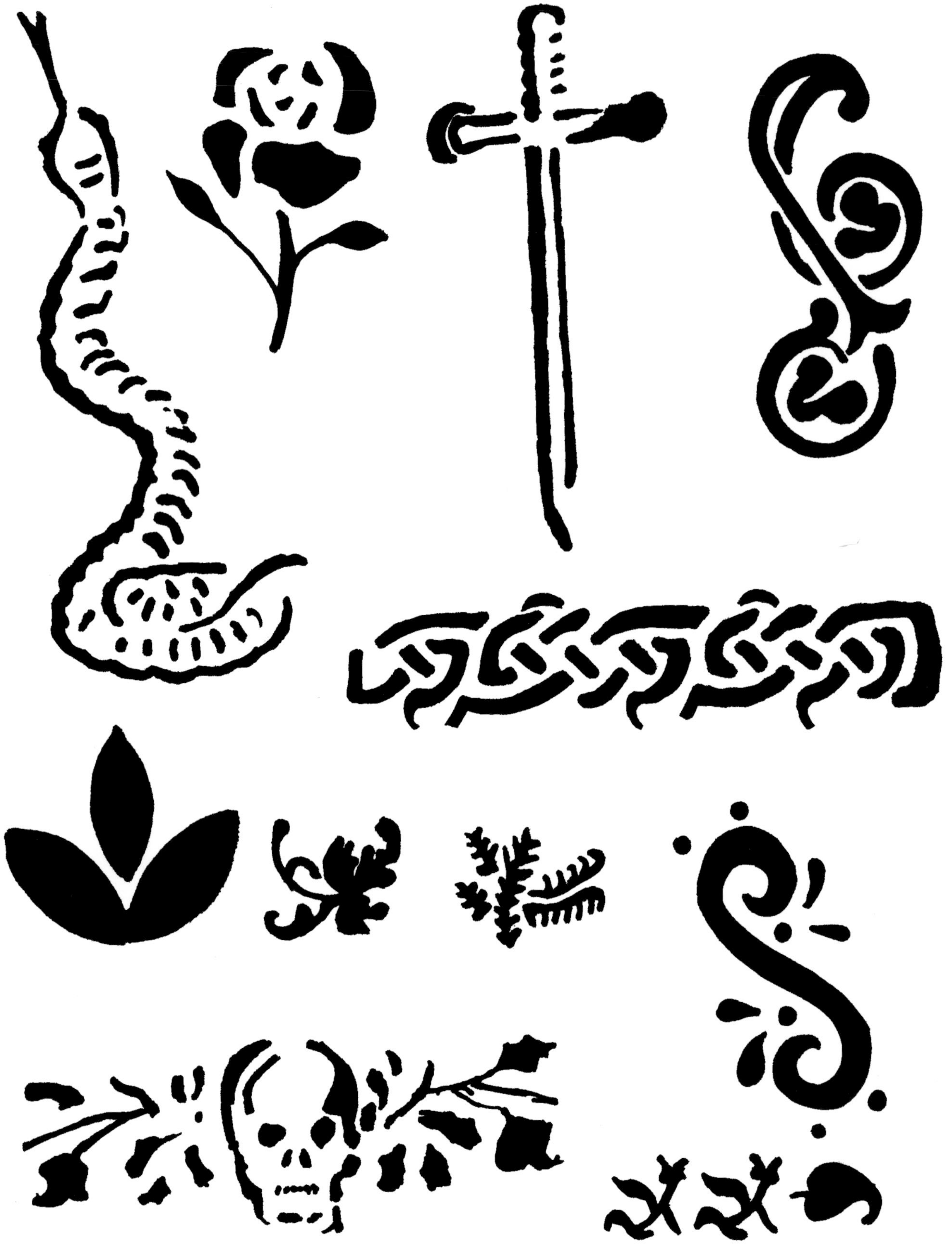

Painting Airbrush Stencil Tattoos

Fish

1 Make the fish stencil, place on arm, and airbrush black paint in the cut-out spaces. Use face paint or acrylic paint to fill in the color of any of these stencils.

2 Using the medium brush and face paint, make long tapering strokes for the sea grass. Paint the tail section.

3 Using the small brush and yellow face or acrylic paint, fill in the neck section, eye, and mouth. When the green paint is dry paint over some ends of the grass with yellow, letting it blend with the green. Do the same for the green in the tail section.

Chess Piece

1 Make the stencil for chess piece, cutting out spaces to be black. Place on leg. Airbrushing black. Remove stencil.

2 Using a small brush and white face or acrylic paint, fill in the spaces.

Swan

1 Make the stencil for the swan and cut out the entire design. Place on leg. Airbrush the cut-out space with black. Remove stencil.

Caduceus with Wings

1 Make the stencil for the caduceus and cut out the black areas of the design. Place on leg.

2 Airbrush the cut-out space black. Remove stencil.

3 Using medium brush and white face or acrylic paint fill in the wings.

4 Using the small brush and yellow face or acrylic paint, fill in the bodies of snakes.

Top Hat

1 Make the top hat and cane stencil, cutting out the entire design. Place on leg.

2 Airbrush the cut-out space. Remove stencil. While still wet, blot a space on the front of hat, as shown.

3 Using the small brush and white face paint, make ends of cane white. Make white streak on top of hat.

4 Using the same brush and red face paint, outline brim of hat and band.

Pumpkin

1 Make the pumpkin stencil cutting out all black areas around pumpkin body. Place on leg.

2 Airbrush the cut-out space black. Remove stencil.

3 With a small brush and orange paint, fill in the pumpkin body.

4 With a small brush and green paint, make grass and leaves.

Skull

1 Make the skull stencil, cutting out all black areas on the design. Place on leg.

2 Airbrush the cut-out spaces black. Remove stencil.

3 Using the medium brush and white paint, fill in the skull areas.

Aztec Anklet

1 Make the ankle stencil by cutting out all the black areas of the design. Place on ankle.

2 Airbrush the cut-out areas black. Remove the stencil.

3 Using the small brush and turquoise paint, fill in the open spaces of the design.

Snake

1 Make the snake stencil, cutting out all the black areas on the pattern. Place on leg.

2 Airbrush cut-out areas black. Remove stencil.

3 Using small brush and yellow paint, make yellow strokes, as shown.

4 Using the same brush and dark orange paint, make orange strokes beside yellow strokes and forked tongue.

Tropical Fish

1 Make the tropical fish stencil cutting out the black outline and black areas. Place on arm.

2 Airbrush cut-out areas black.

3 Using a medium brush and yellow paint, fill in the head area and middle body part.

4 Using the same brush and blue paint, fill in back body part and eye.

Butterfly

1 Make the butterfly stencil, cutting out the black outline and any other black areas on the pattern. Place on ankle

2 Airbrush the cut-out areas black. Remove stencil.

3 Using the small brush and pink paint, fill in wings.

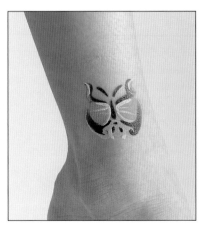

4 Using the same brush and blue paint, fill in bottom part of butterfly.

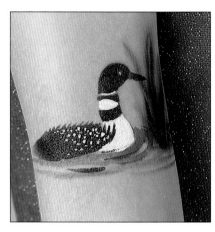

Loon

1 Make the loon stencil, cutting out all the black areas on the pattern. Place on arm.

2 Airbrush the cut-out areas black. Remove the stencil.

3 Using a medium brush and white paint, fill in body area and reeds.

4 Using a small brush and brown paint, make reeds and eye.

5 Using the same brush and gray paint, make sweeping strokes under duck for water ripples. Go over some ripples with blue paint.

Orca

1 Make the orca stencil, cutting out the orca outline. Place on leg. Airbrush black.

2 Using small brush and white paint, fill in orca body.

3 Using the medium brush and blue paint, make water splashes.

4 Using the same brush and white paint, outline water splashes.

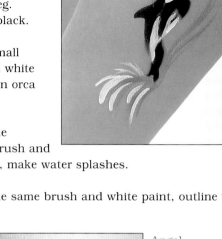

Long Caduceus

1 Make the caduceus stencil by cutting out the entire design. Place on leg.

2 Airbrush the cut-out area black. Remove stencil.

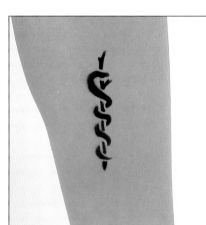

Angel

1 Make the angel stencil by cutting out the black areas of the design. Place on arm.

2 Airbrush the cut-out areas black. Remove stencil.

3 Using a medium brush and white paint, fill in the open areas of the design.

Rose

1 Make the rose stencil, cutting out the rose outline. Place on ankle. Airbrush black.

2 Using small brush and white paint, go over the black outline in the rose petals.

3 Using the medium brush and red paint, fill in the rose section.

Flying Eagle

1 Make the flying eagle stencil by cutting out all black areas on pattern. Place on arm.

2 Airbrush the cut-out parts black. Remove stencil.

3 Using a medium brush and white paint, fill in the uncolored areas.

4 Using the same brush and brown paint touch up part of wings and tail. Make eye yellow.

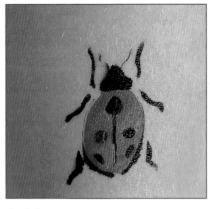

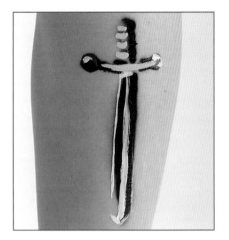

Eagle Head

1 Make the eagle stencil, cutting out the black outline and any other black areas on the pattern. Place on arm.

2 Airbrush the cut-out areas black. Remove stencil.

3 Using the small brush and yellow paint, fill in beak and eyes.

4 Using the medium brush and white paint, fill in eagle head. With the same brush and brown paint, make feathered brush strokes downward from the neck of the eagle.

Ladybug

1 Make the ladybug stencil, cutting out the black areas of the pattern only. Place on arm.

2 Airbrush the cut-out areas black. Remove stencil.

3 Using the medium brush and red paint, fill in the body of the ladybug.

Sword

1 Make the sword stencil by cutting out the black outline of the sword on the pattern. Place on leg.

2 Airbrush the cut-out area black. Remove stencil.

3 Using the same brush and yellow paint, fill in handle and top of sword.

4 Using the same brush and blue paint, fill in blade.

Thistle

1 Make the thistle stencil by cutting out the black outline of the flower and leaves, and other black areas of the pattern. Place on leg.

2 Airbrush the cut-out areas black. Remove stencil.

3 Using medium brush and green paint, fill in the leaves around flower.

4 Using the small brush and purple paint, fill in flower petals. With the same brush and white paint, make light brush strokes at center of flower.

5 With the same brush and yellow-green paint, go over some leaves.

Hearts

1 Make the heart stencil by cutting out all the black areas of the design. Place on ankle or leg several times to get the number of hearts needed.

2 Airbrush the cut-out areas black. Remove the stencil.

3 Using the medium brush and red paint, draw a ribbon joining hearts.

4 With the same brush and white paint make highlight marks around hearts and on hearts.

Design Anklet

1 Make the design stencil by cutting out all the black areas of the pattern.

2 Airbrush the cut-out areas black. Remove the stencil.

3 Using the medium brush and purple paint, fill in the open spaces.

Henna Temporary Tattoos

Henna is a natural product that was used by men and women in ancient Egypt as temporary decoration for nails and feet. The plant *Lawsonia Intermis*, is native to northeastern Africa and yields an orange-red dye still used in the Middle East and East Asia to color hair, fingernails, and the soles of feet. The leaves are dried and ground to a powder that can be mixed in a variety of ways to apply to the area to be colored. The leaves contain a substance that reacts with the keratin of human hair and skin to form the characteristic orange-brown pigment. Applied as a tattoo, the attractive stained design lasts for up to two weeks depending on skin type and the care given to the henna art. Henna is not know to cause any skin irritation but you can do a patch test before you proceed.

Henna art can create fun designs, beautiful jewelry patterns, even logos and abstract figures for children, young adults, men and women. These temporary tattoos can be featured on arms, legs, hands, feet, necks, backs, waists and worn to the beach, to business, or to parties. The striking designs can be small and simple or complex works of art. With a little practice you can make great temporary tattoos on your own skin or on your family and friends.

There are many designs to copy on the following pages. The technique is not difficult but requires practice to perfect. Once you are set up, you can begin to outline the pattern of your choice. Here are some hints how to proceed. Remember that the tattoos take considerable time to dry so be sure to allow sufficient time when you undertake this project.

The henna designs in this book are created freehand by Shahad. He uses skin as his canvas to paint temporary tattoos that are beautiful to look at and fun to wear.

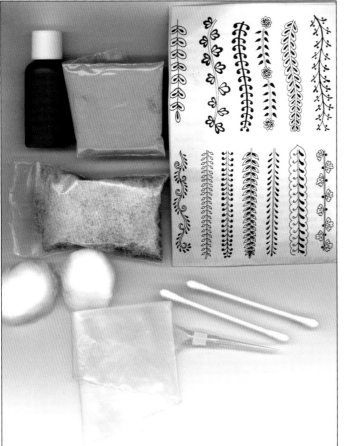

Henna Equipment

1 Purchase the henna of your choice in powder form and follow the directions on the package for handling. Henna is available at East Indian grocery stores or you can order this henna kit (p 96).

2 It is best to mix henna powder in a glass bowl or jar which can be washed afterward. Plastic containers will stain permanently.

3 Mixed henna should sit for 24 hours before using for best results.

4 The mixed henna paste is applied by a cone (in the kit) or you can make your own using a plastic storage bag.

To make cones fold storage bag and slit along fold to make 2 triangles. Each will make 1 cone.

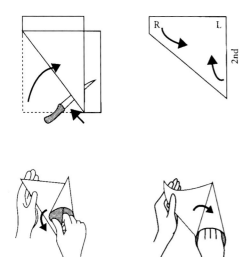

Hold the right point of the triangle in your left hand with the point towards you. In your right hand grasp the right hand point and curl it over until this point touches the apex point.

Hold the 2 points together with your right hand. Grasp the left point with your left hand and wrap the plastic around cone so the point meets the other 2 points. The 3 points should touch leaving no hole at the tip. Secure the edge of the cone inside and out with tape.

Henna Application

Henna Techniques
There are a variety of ways to mix the henna for tattoo art. This one works very well.

1 Mix 2 tsp henna powder with enough water to make a paste of cake-mix consistency. Cover container with plastic wrap and allow to sit at room temperature for 24 hours.

2 Stir mixture and spoon into plastic cone or applicator and seal. Use scissors or a blade to cut the top of the applicator or cone. Make a very small opening so that the henna line you squeeze out will be very fine.

3 Soak a cotton swab with rubbing alcohol or mehndi oil and cleanse skin area where the tattoo is to be applied.

4 Squeeze out the henna to make the pattern. It's like making icing decorations on a cake. Wipe tip constantly with tissue so it won't clog.

5 When design is completed, dry for 15 minutes, then dab lightly with a cotton pad soaked with a mixture of 2 tbs lime juice and 1 tsp sugar. This will darken the color.

6 When henna is dry it will begin to flake off leaving the orange-brown pattern on the skin. Remove dried henna by scraping rather than washing.

7 For optimum results allow henna design to dry for 2 hours, cover it with a dry paper towel, and wrap with plastic wrap overnight. Wash off in the morning.

8 Apply a light coat of oil (sesame, sunflower, olive, baby oil) before and after showering to maintain the color and glow of the henna art.

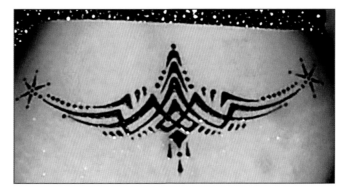

Making Henna Designs

You don't have to be a great artist to create these beautiful designs. Repeating a simple pattern like a dot, a daisy, or a star around an ankle, wrist, or neck will make a very nice henna tattoo. To make the butterfly design prepare the henna using the application of your choice. Prepare the skin (p 74). Begin making the pattern starting with the butterfly wing. Draw the pattern carefully, one small part at a time. Making the pattern is sometimes easier if you draw the design on the skin with chalk line or water-base pencil. Do this before you begin the henna but after you have prepared the skin area with alcohol or mehndi oil. You can use many objects to outline henna patterns such as a glass or bottle top for a circle or a simple star or animal shape that you cut out.

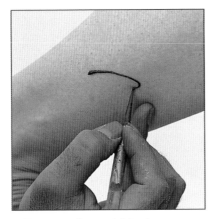

1 Begin making right wing design with an even steady flow of henna.

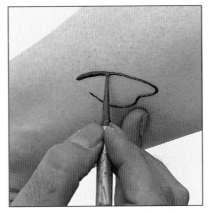

2 Rest pinky finger on skin to help make a steady paint line.

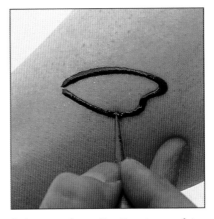

3 A second application is used to broaden and define wing.

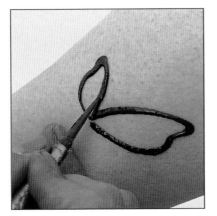

4 Left wing has been drawn smaller and gone over for the second time.

5 Bottom left part of wing is now drawn following same method.

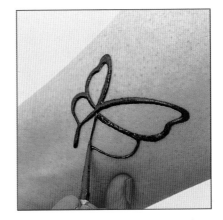

6 Continue drawing final bottom right wing as shown.

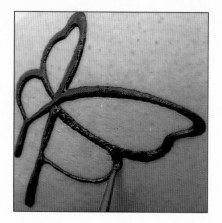

7 Outline the right bottom wing as shown.

8 A wooden orange stick is used to clean excess henna around edges.

9 Body of butterfly is now drawn.

10 Antennae are added next. Be careful not to smudge previously drawn areas.

11 Dots are arranged along inside top wings.

12 Just below dots lines are created next.

13 Fill in area on bottom wings as shown.

14 Lines and a star are created for special effects.

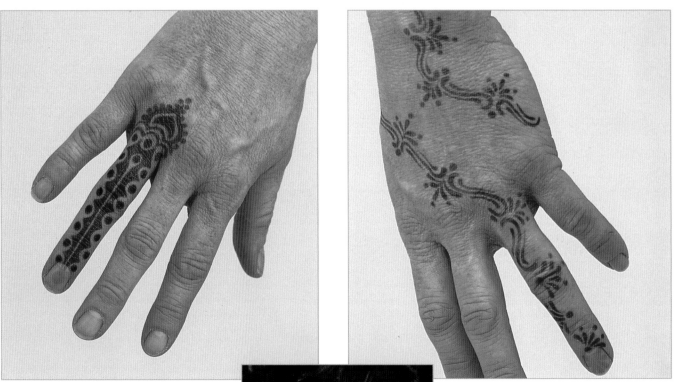

When henna has dried it will flake off leaving the traditional orange-brown colored designs, which will stay on the skin and darken within a couple of days. Designs may last up to two weeks depending on skin type and care given to the henna.

Nail Designs

Painting nails is so much fun and such a special treat. Whether your nails are long or short or somewhere in between, having your nails decorated with color and design is a great way to draw admiring glances. Anyone can wear nail art, no matter what age. As you practice, the design painting becomes easier and you can make your nail decoration suitable for holiday events or parties, for business or just for fun.

Most people prefer freehand painting, but you can purchase stencils for nails and airbrush the paint or you can stick on purchased decals or wear nails that are already painted. The nail designs in this book are all done freehand using nail polish, paint, and some special effects. Some are conservative for business or school. Some are wild and exotic ready for a celebration.

Getting Started

1 Set up the equipment you will need. Purchase nail polish colors at any department store or beauty center. Acrylic paints may be purchased at any department store or craft store.

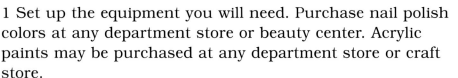

Brush has 7 long hairs drawn to a fine point when wet to make fine lines

2 Also buy several fine brushes, some with short hairs and some with long hairs. Cut off some long hairs on one brush, leaving about 7 hairs, as shown at right. Cut off several hairs on another short-haired brush to make it capable of drawing a fine line.

3 If you wish to use special effects such as glitters or small rhinestones you can purchase them at craft stores.

4 Have a small cardboard or plastic card that can be used as a palette for laying out the paint colors and for mixing colors.

5 Have a small jar of water for cleaning brushes. Use tissue to wipe brushes.

6 Purchase a dotter tool at a beauty supply store or use toothpicks to paint small dots.

7 Gel is used to build some designs. It can be purchased at most department stores.

Painting Nail Designs

Daisy Pattern

1 Make sure nails are an even length and file smooth with an emery board. Push back cuticles. Scrub under nails with a nail brush, soap, and water. Dry hands.

2 Apply base coat nail polish to all nails. Allow to dry.

3 Apply nail polish of your choice (deep wine shown here). Paint one brush stroke down one side of nail, one brush stroke down other side of nail, finish with one brush stroke down center of nail, for smooth, even color. Paint all nails, allow to dry. Paint another coat.

4 Lay out materials for design (daisy shown here). Put dab of white, yellow, green acrylic paint on palette card (top right photo). Replace lids on paint bottles so paint will not dry out.

5 Using dotter tool or toothpick, dip into yellow paint on card and make dot on nail for center of daisy. Repeat for all nails. Clean dotter tool.

6 Dip tool into white paint and make petals around the daisy center, as shown. Make a daisy on each nail. Clean dotter tool.

7 Dip dotter tool into green paint and make stem and leaves for each daisy, as shown. Allow to dry.

8 Apply a coat of clear nail polish on each nail to protect the design. Allow to dry completely.

Star-Burst Pattern

1 Apply base coat nail polish to all nails. Allow to dry.

2 Apply nail polish of your choice (burgundy shown here). Apply two coats. Allow to dry.

3 Lay out brushes, water jar, gold sparkles bottle, and dotter tool. Put dab of white and silver paint together on palette card. Put long streak of gold paint on palette card, as shown.

4 Wet long thin brush in water and draw it through fingers to make a smooth, even line.

5 Draw length of brush through the gold paint on the palette to load brush with paint.

6 Lay the gold carefully across the nail with a steady hand and lift off, leaving long gold line.

7 Make three gold lines at the side of the nail. Repeat for all nails.

8 Clean brush with water. Smooth with fingers. Draw brush through silver mixture on palette. Apply beside gold lines, as shown. Make one or two silver lines. Repeat for all nails.

9 Using gold sparkles paint make a dusting over side of nail. Repeat for all nails, as shown at right.

10 This design is elegant for day or evening wear.

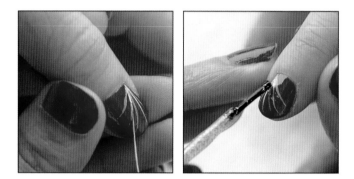

Holiday nails for the triplets

Laura wears dark mauve polish decorated with white snowflakes and silver sparkles.

Stephanie chose eggplant polish decorated with a line of gold and gold sparkles.

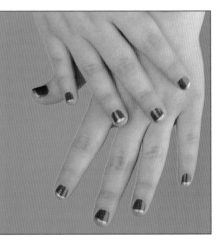

Gillian's nails are painted a plum color with the nail tips painted white.

Try any of these fun designs

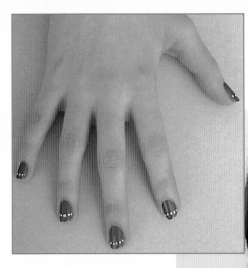

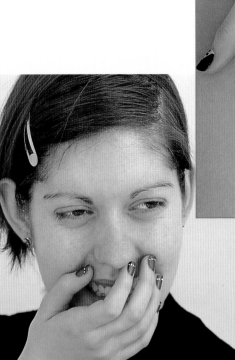

Electric blue

1 Apply base coat.

2 Cover nails with metallic blue nail polish (2 coats).

3 Using the dotter tool or toothpick and white nail polish make a row of dots across nails.

Golden Girl

1 Apply base coat.

2 Cover nails with gold nail polish (2 coats).

3 Paint French tips with bronze metallic polish.

Yin Yang

1 Apply base coat.

2 Cover nails with white nail polish (2 coats).

3 Using black nail polish, color half the nail diagonally.

4 Using a thin brush and black nail polish make marks on white half of nail.

Bow Tie

1 Apply base coat.

2 Cover nails with clear nail polish (2 coats).

3 Paint French tips with white nail polish.

4 Using a fine paintbrush and black polish make tiny bows on each nail.

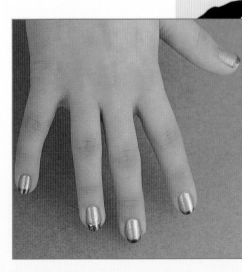

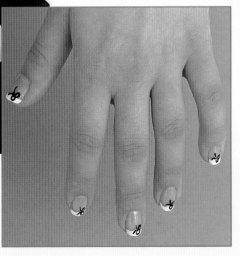

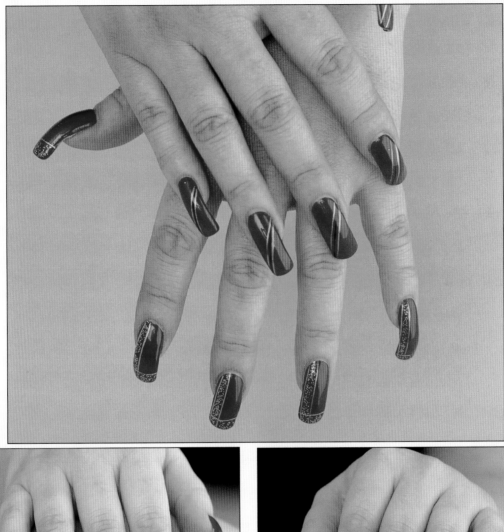

Nails are painted ruby red. The long thin brush is used to paint two gold lines and a black line on each nail.

Use ruby red polish. The long thin brush is used to paint the gold lines on each nail. The spaces are filled in with gold sparkles.

These nail designs are created freehand. Each one is a work of art. With some patience and practice you can do any one of these nail designs and perhaps add a special touch to create your own masterpiece. Nails are colored with nail polish and paint and decorated with sparkles, jewels, and other effects, which can be purchased at department stores, craft stores, or beauty supply shops.

Modern Miss

1 Apply base coat.

2 Apply gray polish (2 coats).

3 Make 5 dark blue paint lines.

4 Make 5 white paint lines.

5 Decorate with dark blue, gray, and gold sparkle polishes.

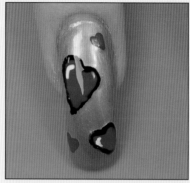

Heart Throb

1 Apply base coat.

2 Apply gray polish (2 coats).

3 Make black paint outline of 2 large hearts.

4 Use red paint for large and small hearts.

5 Use white paint for highlights on 2 large hearts.

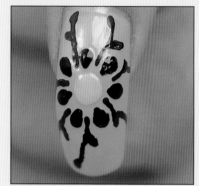

Sunflower

1 Base coat polish.

2 Apply yellow polish (2 coats).

3 Use black paint for leaves and vines.

4 Use lighter yellow paint for center of flower.

At the Beach

1 Apply base coat.

2 Paint nails teal color (2 coats).

3 Use skin tone color for sand.

4 Use brown paint for palm tree trunk and light brown for footprints.

5 For palm leaves use 2 tones of green (darker for the back).

6 Use white paint for clouds.

7 Use blue paint for water.

8 Use white paint for white caps on water.

9 Use yellow paint for sun painted on finger over beach scene.

Purple Patch

1 Apply base coat.

2 Gold polish (2 coats) covers nail.

3 Use black paint lines to outline pattern.

4 Make purple paint design.

5 Finish with silver sparkle polish.

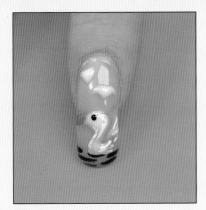

Swan

1 Apply base coat.

2 Use white paint for clouds (2 coats).

3 Use white paint to create body, head, and wing of swan.

4 Black paint for eyes.

5 Use blue paint for water lines.

6 Use whiter white to highlight swan.

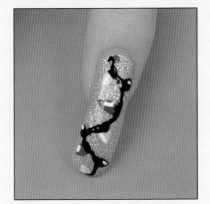

Christmas Lights

1 Apply base coat.

2 Apply silver sparkle polish (2 coats).

3 Use black paint for light cord.

4 Use red paint for 3 light bulbs.

5 Use blue paint for 3 light bulbs.

6 Use yellow paint for 3 light bulbs.

7 Use white paint for highlights.

Rudolph

1 Apply base coat.

2 Apply silver sparkle polish (2 coats).

3 Use dark brown paint for head, snout, and antlers.

4 Use red paint for nose.

5 Use light brown paint for highlights.

6 A dab of paint secures eyes.

7 Use dark brown paint for nostrils.

Fish Bowl

1 Apply base coat.

2 Apply blue polish (2 coats).

3 Apply green paint for grass.

4 Use brown paint for grass.

5 Use yellow paint for 1 big fish, and 2 small fish.

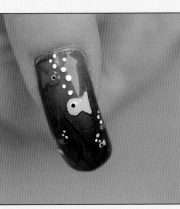

6 Use red paint for 1 big fish, and 2 small fish.

7 Use white paint for eye.

8 Use black paint for small dot in eye.

9 Use white paint for bubbles.

Santa Claus

1 Apply base coat.

2 Apply blue sparkle polish (2 coats).

3 Use face color paint for face.

4 Use green paint for eyes with dot of black paint.

5 Use black paint for mouth.

6 Use pink paint for nose.

7 Use white paint for hair and beard.

8 Paint hat and body red.

9 Use black paint for lines of arms and mitts.

10 Use white paint dot for hat tassel and cuffs.

11 Use gold paint for buttons and buckle.

12 Make black paint dot in buckle.

Party Nails

These fun designs are painted on real nails. You can choose any one for all your nails depending on the occasion. The part of the design painted on the skin will last only a day and will have to be repainted or you can modify the design to be contained only on the nail.

Business Nails

Simply Elegant

1 Apply base coat.

2 Cover nails with deep plum nail polish.

3 Using the brush with long hairs and leaving a little space from sides of the nail apply one thin black paint line vertically. Leaving a little space from the tip of the nail apply the second thin black line horizontally. Both lines should meet below the tips of the nail.

4 Using the dotter tool or small brush and black paint draw two squares at the end of each black joining line.

Exotic Art

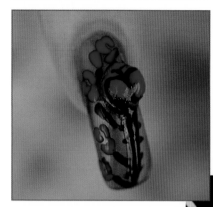

Rose

1 Apply base coat.

2 Cover the nails with green nail polish (2 coats).

3 Use nail polish to build up the rose shape. Allow to dry.

Flower

1 Apply base coat.

2 Cover the nail with metallic purple nail polish (2 coats).

3 Use nail polish to build up the flower and leaves.

4 Make the stem with nail polish. Allow to dry.

5 Paint the rose red.

6 Paint smaller red roses around large rose.

7 Paint the stems green.

8 Paint black highlights on the rose.

Ladybug

1 Apply base coat (2 coats).

2 Paint green grass stems using long-haired brush.

4 Use nail glue to place large jewel at center of flower and 2 smaller jewels around top and bottom of flower.

5 Paint blue shading on flower and blue at the base of the nail.

6 Paint yellow surrounding the flower.

Daisy

1 Apply base coat.

2 Cover the nail with metallic purple nail polish (2 coats).

3 Make large daisy petals.

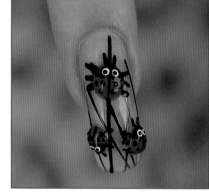

3 Make ladybug shapes with nail polish.

4 Paint ladybug red.

5 Paint black heads and dots.

6 Use dotter tool or toothpick to paint black antenae and legs.

7 Use dotter tool to paint white eyes and black dot in eyes.

4 Use nail glue to place large jewel at center of daisy.

5 Paint white petals for the daisy.

6 Paint white daisies at the base of the nail.

7 Use the dotter tool or toothpick to paint yellow centers.

8 Paint light blue sparkles.

Note These sculptured nail designs were created with gel which can be purchased at department stores or beauty supply stores. Acrylic sculpture kits are also available.

Grapes

1 Apply base coat.

2 Cover the nail with fushia nail polish (2 coats).

3 Use nail polish to form the balls for ten grapes.

4 Paint one bunch of grapes green.

5 Paint other bunch of grapes purple.

6 Paint green stems and leaves.

7 Paint dark green highlights on one side of grapes.

8 Paint white highlights on other side of grapes.

Bird feather

1 Apply base coat.

2 Cover the nail with light gray polish (2 coats).

3 Use the brush with the long hair to lay long black lines on the nail to make a spine for the feathers.

4 Paint black dots in the feathering pattern with the dotter tool or a toothpick.

5 Paint the white feather pattern.

Tiger pattern

1 Apply base coat.

2 Cover the nail with gold nail polish (2 coats).

3 Use fine brush to paint black stripes.

4 Highlight the stripes with brown paint.

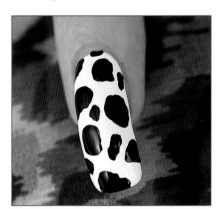

Cow pattern

1 Apply base coat.

2 Cover the nail with white nail polish (2 coats).

3 Use dotter tool or small brush to paint black patches.

Leopard pattern

1 Apply base coat.

2 Cover the nail with gold nail polish (2 coats).

3 Paint black spots.

4 Highlight the spots with brown paint.

Zebra pattern

1 Apply base coat.

2 Cover the nail with white nail polish (2 coats).

3 Use the dotter tool or toothpick to paint black lines.

Toes are Fun

Pampering your feet is the ultimate luxury. Why not give yourself a pedicure and decorate your toenails. Painted toes are great for the beach and show off in sandals too! Choose a design to match your occasion.

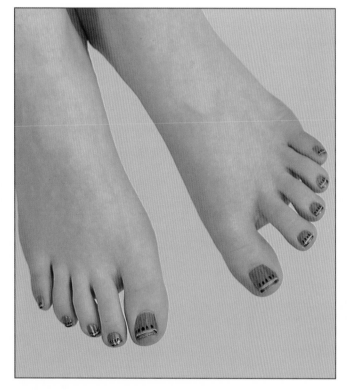

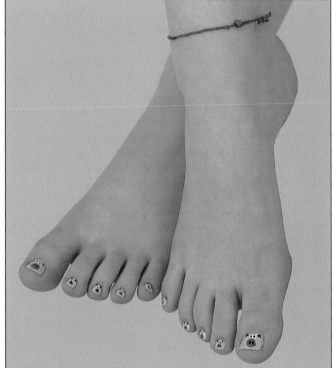

Watermelon slices are ready for summer

1 Apply base coat.

2 Cover nail with red nail polish

3 Paint dark green lines across tips of nails for watermelon skin.

4 Paint a light green line across nails just below dark green line for contrast.

5 Using the black polish and dotter tool or toothpick make small dots for seeds.

These little pigs enjoy being out and about

1 Apply base coat.

2 Cover nail with pink nail polish

3 Paint red circle on the center of the nail for the snout.

4 Using white paint make two small circles above red circle.

5 Using black paint and dotter tool or toothpick paint black dots for eyes, ears, and snout.

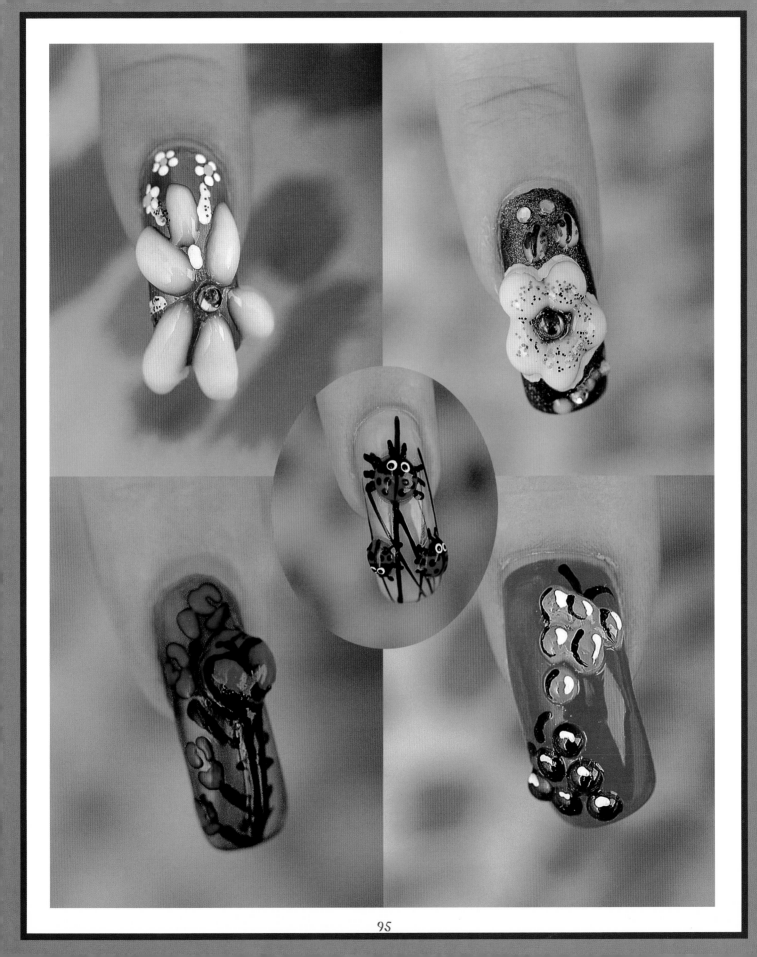

Index

Contacts for further information
Tom Andrich
email hogshair@yahoo.ca

Shahab
Seven Seas International
Box 34084 Winnipeg Canada R3T 5T5
email shahab@doyawannahenna.com
website doyawannahenna.com

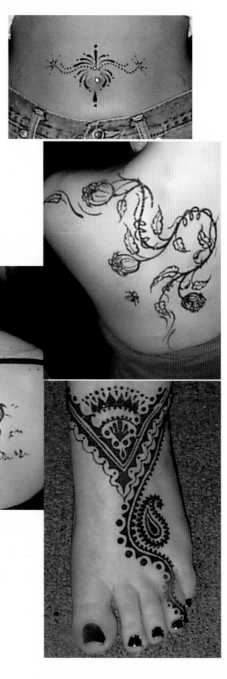